NAVIGATING BPD:

THE ULTIMATE SURVIVAL GUIDE FOR LIVING WITH BORDERLINE PERSONALITY DISORDER

BY

CARONIQUE DECIUS

ISBN 978-976-97561-0-6 (Paperback)

ISBN 978-976-97561-1-3 (E-Book)

Book Cover & Design by Nik Barnes, The Barnes Group, Nassau, The Bahamas.

Editing by T.L. Clarke, Nassau, The Bahamas.

Formatting by Stephanie Brown, Brown Publishing, USA.

Printed in the U.S.A.

First Edition 2025.

Published by Caronique Decius

For permissions, contact:

Caronique Decius, P.O. Box, N-3711, Nassau, The Bahamas

caronique@navigatingbpd.com

Visit: www.navigatingbpd.com

ACKNOWLEDGEMENTS

I would like to thank everyone that helped to bring this book to life and offered me guidance and support in the way that only they could especially:

Kerri, Thomas, Deishay, Tracy “Tray Money”, Th’Mars

and Tia.

For:

JPAN, Asia & AJ

TABLE OF CONTENTS

INTRODUCTION

If you are reading this book, it is likely that you have recently been diagnosed with Borderline Personality Disorder. Finally, there is an explanation for the intense mood swings, the troubled relationships, feelings of emptiness and the loss of sense of self. Receiving the borderline personality diagnosis is scary, yet it is a relief to know that you finally have an answer for the behaviors that you've been displaying. I'm sure that you have long thought that something was wrong, however you could not place a finger on it, and you could never quite figure it out. I had been displaying signs of depression officially since I was 12 years old. It's very likely that there were signs before then, but I was not fully aware. At 12, I was called into the guidance counselor's office because it had been "leaked" that I was self-harming. Although I didn't always have access to razors, my mother was diabetic, and I had access to her testing kit. I would use her lancets and repeatedly stick holes into my wrist until I was satisfied with the amount of blood that was draining from my hand. By the time I was 13, I was full on thinking about suicide. I had concocted numerous plans of how I would end my life and at the time I believed that the only care anyone would have would be the financial debt I would leave behind because of my funeral. Even this, I had mitigated by telling my parents that I wanted to be cremated in the event of my death (and no, they did not realize that my saying that was the result of my planning my death). As I got older, I came to the belief that I had to have dysthymia (now called Persistent Depressive Disorder). I was very focused on the depressive symptoms. They really made my life miserable and quite undesirable to say the least.

When I first heard about Borderline Personality Disorder, I knew almost immediately that that's what I had. I say almost only because we were taught not to diagnose ourselves, especially in the absence of formal assessments. But there is something to be said for that moment when the switch goes on and you can say confidently that these are the symptoms that fit me, and I know that THIS is my diagnosis. At the time I was in college and despite the many challenges I faced during that time, it wasn't until after college that I received my diagnosis. In the time between receiving my diagnosis I would have been counseled for an eating disorder, possible bi-polar disorder and eventually medicated for my very prominent depressive symptoms. Fear of abandonment was my tipping point – my closest friend at the time told me that she was unable to come and be with me at a very vulnerable moment. In that moment, I was resolved that I would leave work and hang myself. I knew that if I left work and stepped foot in my house, my life was over. I called the psychologist that I was seeing at the time, and she directed me to come in and see the doctor who was having clinic at the hospital at the same time. He assessed me and sent me down to the ER where I waited to be hospitalized for the first time in my life.

That was 12 years ago, and I have learned a thing or two about the disorder and about mental health in general along the way. This book is a how-to-guide for navigating the roller coaster ride that is BPD. In this book, I will walk you through some of the common experiences of having

BPD, experiences that are seldom spoken about online or that are commonly replaced with gentle euphemisms. I will be preparing you for what is to come in hopes that when these issues do arise, you have some tools in your tool belt to take on the challenge. While I will explain what BPD is and discuss some of the key components of the disorder, this book is not meant to be a workbook, a replacement for treatment or even a book about the different traits of BPD. There's a lot of information on the internet about the traits of BPD and the subtypes and lots of books that discuss the different facets of the diagnosis. What I aim to do here is to give you the autonomy to take treatment into your own hands, and instead of equipping you with general information, give you insights into the disorder that are not readily available outside of experience. Although I am trained in psychology, I want to give you insights into BPD as a patient and not a professional. Therefore, I say to you, you will still need your psychologist and/or psychiatrist, specialist or primary care doctor. You will also still need to purchase a workbook (if that is what you so desire) and you will need to continue treatment. I will not be providing treatment rather holding your hand as you undergo treatment. With that said, let's jump in!

WHAT IS BORDERLINE PERSONALITY DISORDER?

Borderline Personality Disorder is a mental illness that mainly impacts one's ability to manage one's emotions. A Personality Disorder is not a mental illness in the traditional way that we think when we think of mental illnesses. Traditionally, we think of mood disorders like depression, anxiety, bipolar disorder etc. We even sometimes think of psychotic disorders like schizophrenia, schizoaffective disorder and disorders where one experiences a "break in reality". BPD falls under what is known as a *Personality Disorder.* Personality disorders are a set of traits that are embedded into our characters over time. They affect the way that we see and experience the world. A psychiatrist, Dr. Tracey Marks, explained this best by saying that a personality disorder is like the climate, whereas a mood disorder is like the weather. The weather changes from day to day and even hour to hour based on the environment. The climate, however, remains quite stable and does not vary much. As I am from a Caribbean Island, I understand that well. Here, in the Bahamas sometimes rainy, and other times rainy to the point of flooding; sometimes it's sunny, and other times sunny to the point of heat waves; sometimes breezy while other times the trees seem to stand motionless. Overall, our climate is hot and humid. No matter what the weather conditions are, it is almost always hot! The heat stays consistent. Then when the cold air descends on the hot air, there is a hurricane. The climate is such that, actual cold cannot thrive here. Personality disorders are similar such that our moods are like the weather and our personality is like the climate. Despite the mood - sad, angry, happy, you name it - we still experience a stable and consistent level of disturbance. Because it is a part of who we are and how we see and interact with the world, there is only the ability to manage the symptoms. I like to call it a stable instability. I will speak more about the traits of that instability.

Now that we understand the stability and consistency of a personality disorder, we can talk about the nine (9) hallmark traits of BPD. You only need to display five of the nine traits to be diagnosed with Borderline Personality Disorder, therefore, you may not be able to directly relate to all nine traits.

1) Unstable or shifting self-image - You may find that your view of yourself changes from time to time. It is not simply imposter syndrome – which is the belief that you are less capable than you are in reality. Sometimes you find yourself very proud of who you are and what you've accomplished and other times you find it hard to believe that you've done anything worthy of praise or commendation. Sometimes it's physical whereas you can look in the mirror and feel great about yourself and your body and then it changes whereas you cannot bear to look at yourself in the mirror at all. The way that you are experiencing yourself in the moment can dictate the way you handle internal and external conflicts and interactions.

2) Unstable interpersonal relationships - You may find yourself in a plethora of relationships and friendships because it is difficult

to maintain long lasting relationships usually based on fear of abandonment and the unstable balance between idealizing and devaluing a person. You may also find it hard to build trust which also affects how you handle relationships. A combination of these factors can impact the volatility of your relationships.

3) Mood swings - In addition to our unsteady climate, our weather frequently changes. It is quite likely that what may have gotten you into treatment is your mood. BPD is commonly misdiagnosed as bi-polar disorder because of the constant mood swings. It is important to note that while we do experience mood swings, they are not as scheduled/regulated as someone with bi-polar disorder. This means that you can't steadily track that the mood swings happen every six weeks to two months or once a quarter. They are more varied and irregular.

4) Impulsivity/Self-destructive behavior - Our mood swings are consistent and very intense (there is evidence that we experience our emotions more intensely and for longer periods of time compared to neurotypical persons). As a result of this, we tend to do things to relieve the intense emotions which usually involves impulsive behaviors such as drinking excessive amounts of alcohol, being promiscuous (usually in an attempt secure some form of attachment), taking dangerous drugs and engaging in other dangerous behaviors with very little thought or consideration.

5) Fear of rejection and abandonment - People with BPD tend to be very sensitive to real or perceived abandonment. It is very

common for individuals with BPD to have experienced emotional neglect in their childhood or even physical abandonment. Perceiving that someone has removed their affection or love triggers intense emotions. Rejection is also a sensitive trigger as it plays on not being good enough to receive that love and affection, this can be exacerbated by our current state of sense of self/self-image.

6) Self-harm & Suicidal tendencies - People with BPD tend to suffer great emotional pain coupled with the inability to regulate that pain. As a result, we try to escape it through substances or ending our lives entirely. Suicide is frequently an option for escaping the steady and consistent emotional pain we endure. Self-harm is also frequently used as a means of regulating the intense emotions. However, in many cases these methods are used to express pain and garner support. It can be used as a form of "manipulation" to get the help and attention we need, as we tend to be ill-equipped in healthily requesting help for a number of reasons.

7) Explosive rage - The intensity of emotions plays a major role in this trait as it can cause a *seemingly* larger than appropriate response to negative stimuli that triggers rage. There are four different sub-types of BPD, and they all tend to express some level of rage both internally and externally (which I will expand on in the next section). The most common factor across all sub-types is the general idea that the rage is triggered by something *seemingly* small or *relatively* insignificant. (It is worth noting that the reaction is, in fact, in proportion to your emotions but seems inappropriate to those around you.)

8) Chronic feelings of emptiness - People that struggle with BPD tend to suffer with persistent feelings of emptiness which can be described in two ways. One way is having a feeling of deep longing. Imagine a bucket with a large hole in the bottom; there is a constant longing and yearning for love and attention and affection that cannot be filled no matter how hard you try. The second way is a physical feeling of having a gaping hole in your body where your purpose, passion and fulfillment should be, but it's empty. Due to the issues with self-image, it is very difficult to develop a "whole" self that feels fulfilled. Unfortunately, this feeling is chronic.

9) Dissociation and/or Paranoia - This is the psychological term for loss of touch with reality. In times of severe stress people with BPD can detach from reality and experience lapses in memory and/or control. Dissociation can take the form of feeling that you have left your body and are watching what is unfolding but are unable to control or gain access to your body. I liken it to "the sunken place" in the movie "Get Out". You are fully aware of what is taking place but are unable to cognitively engage. Another way you can experience dissociation is when you "check out" mentally and are not fully there. You are acting, behaving and going through the motions based on rote behaviors, however you are not present. Your mind may completely check out whereas you remember nothing, or it may be that your mind is stuck on a thought or feeling while your body is present and conducting everyday life. There is also paranoia, which is typically stress related. It can show up in the form of thinking people are talking about you or are out to get you or harm you in some way. These

symptoms tend to show themselves usually only under extreme stress or when triggered or reminded of an extremely distressing event.

Remember that these are hallmark traits of Borderline Personality Disorder and not an exhaustive list of symptoms. Your symptoms are likely to fall under the umbrella of one of these nine traits. Also, you do not need to possess all nine of these traits to be diagnosed with BPD. The requirement for diagnosis is five of the traits. The next thing I will say is one of the most important in BPD. Everyone experiences BPD differently!

Borderline Personality has four sub-types. They all have the same nine hallmarks but the way you experience them is what will help you to understand what sub-type you have. These sub-types are not actual diagnoses, they are for the sake of helping us to understand the differences we experience.

THE FOUR SUB-TYPES OF BPD

1) *Discouraged/quiet/vulnerable*: Depending on where you do your research, you will find one of those 3 names listed. I tend to use the name "quiet BPD". For reference, this is the one that I identify with most. The reason the experts call it by those names is because of the characteristics. This sub-type tends to experience their symptoms more quietly. The intense emotions, rage and anger and the like are usually experienced inwardly. The self-talk is very negative, the outward expressions of discontent are very limited, and they tend to inflict the pain they feel on themselves. Self-harm is more likely in this sub-type. We may hold down jobs well and for longer periods of time and are considered "high functioning". However, the internal battle is very intense and experienced with very little outward expression (tantrums, arguments, conflicts etc.). We tend to be more lonely, isolated and feel empty most of the time. We also fear abandonment to a greater extent. Again, in relation to the other sub-type, our outward expression of this pain is relatively well hidden. Because of the inward and silenced pain this sub-type is frequently misdiagnosed as major depression.

2) *Impulsive*: The impulsive sub-type is very reminiscent of their name. Once triggered, they tend to handle that pain in very impulsive ways like getting drunk to the point of aggression, doing drugs with people whom you aren't certain are safe, unprotected sex with strangers, fast or reckless driving or putting themselves in unsafe positions or places. Another category of the impulsivity is binge behaviors like binge eating, overspending and the like. It's important to note that the aggression doesn't always have to be induced by alcohol or drugs. Being triggered could lead to yelling fits, punching walls or other objects, breaking objects as well. The idea behind this is that the impulsive behavior could be harmful to self or others while there is very little or no regard to the consequences of the action. For example, I have hurt my hand several times by punching objects (walls, stacks of files, doors etc.) without regard for the fact that I could fracture my hand. The main thought is getting the feeling out rather than what consequences come because of the way I go about it. Because of their explosive and unpredictable behavior coupled with being easily irritated, this sub-type is often mistaken as anti-social personality disorder.

3) *Petulant*: This sub-type also shows their emotions outwardly. They tend to fear loss of control and uncertainty more, which can make them present as very demanding, controlling and even manipulative. Their behaviors tend to be more passive-aggressive, and their moods swing greatly and frequently. Their personality seems...well...petulant (or crotchety). This sub-type can be very displeased in their interpersonal relationships, so they try to control them in ways that are often deemed

manipulative, abusive and lacking in boundaries and remorse. However, the root of the problem usually stems from feeling unloved and unworthy. Trying to mitigate those feelings causes a self-fulfilling prophecy. This sub-type also leads to heavy drug and alcohol use. The petulant sub-type can also be mistaken for narcissistic personality.

4) *Self-Destructive*: This sub-type is self-explanatory. This usually manifests as a deep self-hatred or self-loathing and an inability to cope with the inner conflict. Self-destructive behaviors tend to surface through cutting, burning, threats of suicide and suicide attempts, drug use, and adrenaline seeking behaviors. The core of this sub-type is to escape the constant loop of pain and self-loathing by doing and engaging in any kind of behavior that will distract them. Because of the behaviors they engage in, they may also have periods of euphoria where they are, seemingly successfully, running away from their inner turmoil. Because of this, this sub-type is often misdiagnosed as bi-polar disorder.

Now that I've provided a bit more information about Borderline Personality Disorder and the sub-types you are more equipped to understand where you land in the big circle that encompasses us all. Once again it is very important to note that you can fall into more than 1 sub-type and that you may even have a few traits from each group. It's also important to note that BPD is frequently misdiagnosed in general, your misdiagnosis may help you to understand where you fall in terms of a sub-type however, it may not.

Misdiagnoses happen often due to health care providers trying to find a label that fits and helps to guide them in treatment options.

Because BPD is still shrouded in so many questions and uncertainty, you may find yourself being placed in a more contained box that has more research and more answers because it's a bit easier for them to navigate. BPD also commonly has a co-morbid or co-occurring disorder. By this I mean that you can have more than one diagnosis. I have major depression with anxiety alongside my borderline diagnosis. The signs of depression were seen before it was recognized that I had BPD. Borderline Personality is often misdiagnosed as bi-polar disorder however, having both of those disorders are possible and is called border-polar.

Now that that's squared away, I would like to state what this book aims to do. Over the last 12 years of having been diagnosed, I have picked up a thing or two that you won't find online or that is rarely talked about. In some cases, no amount of Reddit forums, Instagram posts or Tik Tok videos you go through will be enough to help you learn these things and in other cases, some people may mention something, but you don't realize how much it applies to you. This book aims to help you fill in those gaps. I've learned there's a specific way to talk to your doctor that gets them to listen to you more readily. I've also learned there are symptoms that you may experience that make your internal struggle much more difficult. Now, while I can't treat those symptoms for you, I can let you know what it is you're looking for and put you on guard of what will be important. I'll be giving you the proverbial cheat sheet of BPD. Because BPD presents itself so differently, I won't be able to touch every single needed piece of information, nor will I be able to speak directly to your specific needs. Therefore, this book is not a substitute for professional treatment, medication, or the like. Also, this book is not a workbook so you will not be getting writing prompts or focus points. I strongly suggest that you keep up with your doctor's and/or therapy appointments and order any workbooks that you think may be helpful.

In this book, I will be walking you through things that tend to only come with time and experience. My hope is to optimize your journey by cutting that learning time. Together, we will navigate the world of BPD.

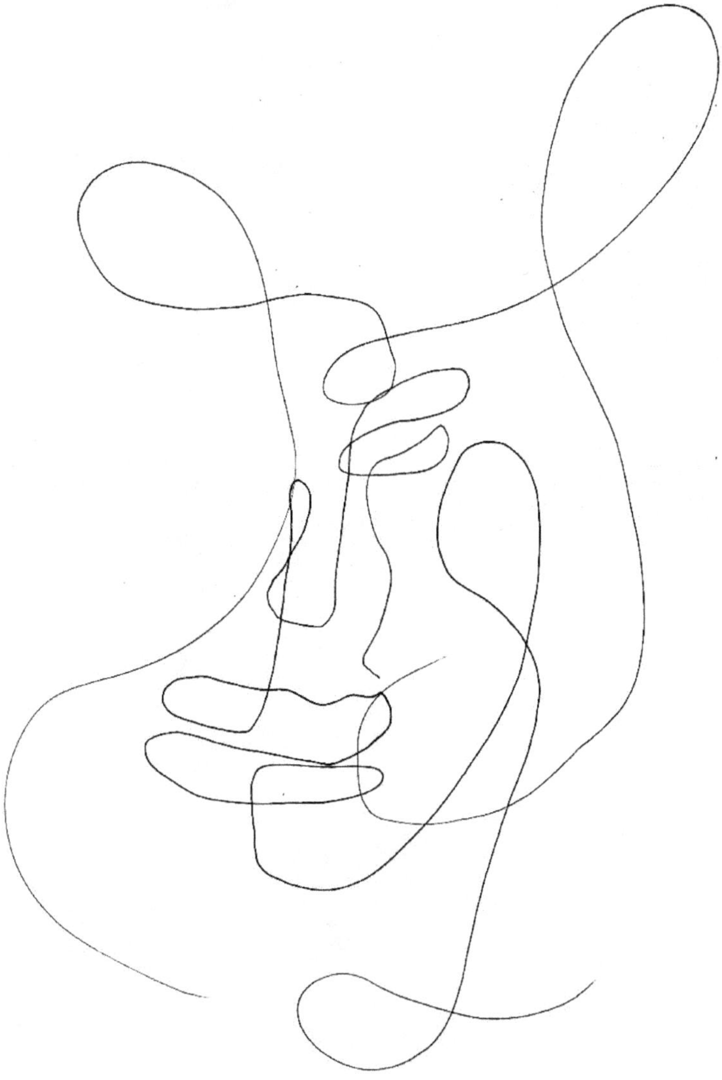

Section 1:

BE YOUR BIGGEST ADVOCATE

Chapter 1:

TALKING TO YOUR DOCTOR

The reality of this chapter is going to hit you like a ton of bricks so there's no other way to address it than to be candid. I want to open by saying doctors are usually in the profession because they want to help. In most cases they are thinking of your welfare and your best interest. Ultimately, they want to do right by you. However, you will meet doctors who will dismiss you, demean you, devalue you and just downright ignore and gaslight you. I've seen it happen so many times where a doctor just didn't care to deal with a patient and their response is less than dignified. When I was hospitalized (I think for the first time), there was another lady on the ward who had bipolar disorder. The way the ward was set up was that there was a small office on the outside in the back of the yard. Outside the office there were benches set up where family members and patients would wait to see the doctor and the space was covered and closed in by faux wood slates. The patients on the ward could only use the space if the nurses had removed the lock to open it up in preparation for the doctors and visitors. While I was there, once the space was opened, I would go and sit on the bench and read a book because it was significantly quieter than being off to the side with the other patients and the ward itself was extremely cold. One day as I'm sitting and reading - a few outpatients and family members had already arrived - the lady with bi-polar disorder came and was very happy because she was expecting to be discharged. She spoke kindly to everyone and started saying her farewells and giving words of encouragement to those of us that would be staying. Once she had gone in with the doctors, they had obviously told her that she was not going to be released, and she was upset to say the least. Behind the door we all heard a very audible "WHAT THE FUCK!" Not long after she left the room, visibly upset and she paced around a bit talking, swearing, blowing off steam. Despite that her behavior was not extreme, it was understandable and showed great restraint and control, they ordered that she be taken to the "side room" and given a sedative. The side room is technically an isolation room. It's off to the side, "safe" and is where they put patients who are violent or out of control. This was not the case with this lady.

After seeing that I vowed to be on my best behavior when talking to the doctors because I didn't want to be victimized in any sense of the word for simply expressing myself. Armed with this experience, I had numerous visits with the doctors where each time I talked to them, explained side effects or discussed situations or voiced displeasure, they would talk over me, dismiss me, "mansplain" (doctorsplain) things to me and completely and consistently refused to listen to me. Now, generally I'm a very agreeable person, very soft-spoken and an introvert if there ever was one. However, once I've been crossed enough, I have the ability to turn the agreeable switch off and voice my discontent. One day, I'd had it, and I went into my appointment quite cross and unwilling to put up with the dismissive attitude of the doctors. I spoke very firmly and plainly about my discomfort, my side effects and my circumstances. When I walked out of the office, there was a clear plan of how to address the side effects and possibly switch medications, I received help from the social worker and follow-up with the psychologist. I remember distinctly thinking "I need to be mad in order for them to listen to me?"

It hurts me, the numerous stories that I've heard of people with similar experiences. There are doctors who refuse to listen, are dismissive, deem you crazy, unstable or are simply just not knowledgeable. I've also had several experiences where if I was agreeable, timid or soft-spoken for any reason, I was completely run over. Then on the flip side if I presented a level of anger that they deemed inappropriate, I would be completely ignored and/or cast aside and not receive the help I needed. Between myself and other mentally ill friends, I have been privy to seeing, hearing and experiencing levels of doctor ego and pride that are astoundingly disgusting. Although it is sad to have to say, in order to have a relatively smooth journey, you *will* have to learn how to talk to your doctor in a way that helps them to hear you. You must be a strong unwavering advocate for yourself and the help you need.

TIPS:

1) The first thing you want to do when talking to your doctor is assume a posture of contentment or confidence. If you have been recently diagnosed, you may not know much about the disorder and haven't come around to doing your own research and so you are relying heavily on what information they give you. If this is the case, you want to stay away from being timid,

shy, ignorant or in general like a damsel in distress. Even though you are relying on them for help, listen to what is said and pick on the information so you can ask questions and make connections with and in front of them. You want to give the impression that you are comfortable in your skin and will not be walked on or dismissed.

2) After you've done your own research, make it known that you have. The truth is they will attempt to shoot you out of the air here. They will advise you that a lot of online information is skewed, dripping in stigma and has a great potential to be false and erroneous. While that is quite true, not everything you would have learned will be wrong or be far from the truth. All mental illness is expressed differently because of individual differences and circumstances and that couldn't be truer than with BPD. As such you may find some information that relates to you that the doctors may not have heard of or experienced before. The point is that you want to show that you are doing the work, you are willing to learn and even more so that you want their help to fill in the gaps.

3) If you are displeased for any reason, make it known. Whether the side effects are too much for you to handle, or you don't think you're getting better, perhaps you think you need more help than what is currently being offered - whatever the case maybe - you want to be very clear about the situation. If you say nothing and then pop up one day saying you're putting your foot down on a matter, it will only come across as you being erratic and non-compliant. Unfortunately, and perhaps even unfairly, this will in turn give them reason to dismiss you.

Furthermore, there will be no documentation of your complaints and therefore no case for helping you with the issue.

4) Be firm. Ultimately this is your mental health journey, and you have to take control of it. If a medication doesn't work, you've complained several times and they won't listen, you present them with the ultimatum that they either change the medication or you will stop taking them, go somewhere else or whatever works for you. Now, keep in mind, they still are professionals and have a reason they thought your mode of treatment would be helpful, but if, and when you have given it a FAIR chance and you find it isn't helpful BE FIRM about your resolve. You do not want to spend more time than necessary in treatment that is counterproductive or just failing.

5) Be Specific. As I mentioned earlier, BPD presents itself in many ways and individual differences make the expression of these symptoms very vast and varied. To get the help you need, be specific about your symptoms, your side effects, medical history, socioeconomic status, family structure, interpersonal relationships and the like. All these things affect your treatment, access to treatment, medications and support. Being specific makes their job easier and your journey smoother.

There are good doctors and not so good doctors, and you may run into both types as you walk this road of BPD. Remember that for the most part, these doctors are here to help. So, whether you don't know much yet or have done some healthy research, you will still have to interact with your doctor to ensure you get the best treatment possible. These tips are here to help you to get the best out of that experience without wasting too much time waiting around for your doctor to respond in a way that is conducive to your needs. The field is undermanned, a lot of them are working in under-resourced hospitals, are overworked and underpaid. While this doesn't give them a right to treat you with anything less than dignity and integrity, it is sometimes understandable that they are tired, burnt out and just doing the best they can. So don't go into it immediately assuming that all doctors are horrible and don't care. Try your best to work with them as they work with you.

Chapter 2:

MEDICATION

In most cases the reason you end up in the hospital or in front of a doctor is a co-morbid disorder or something that requires medication to help level off the severity/intensity of the symptoms. For instance, you may have had significant mood swings and in your euphoric/manic phase you may have been acting recklessly which landed you in hospital. Perhaps your depressive symptoms got so bad that you attempted to take your life which landed you in the hospital or in a seat across from your doctor. Despite how you got there, there's almost an inevitability of being placed on medication. There are a few things you should know and consider when dealing with psychotropic drugs (drugs that alter your mental state).

I mentioned earlier that BPD usually has a co-morbid or co-occurring mood disorder or even an eating disorder. In most cases what gets you into the doctor's office is that co-occurring disorder and being that those symptoms were severe enough to get you in front of a doctor there is a great likelihood that you will need to be placed on medication to help alleviate those symptoms. Think of it this way: You come across a homeless person in need of food, shelter, a bath, haircut, clothes etc. All those needs are symptoms however they are essential. Once you address these basic needs, you are now able to talk with them on a more personal level about what got them on the streets in the first place. Once you do this, you find out that their parent died and they started using substances and lost their job, then their home, then their car and all means of taking care of themselves while actively running away from the grief. You see now that they need grief therapy, substance intervention and community support. It would be much harder to address these problems when you can't talk to them because the stench from their stink is so great, or you can't get past the first few sentences because they're begging for food. They can't be vulnerable when they have no shelter because they don't feel safe at any given moment. The same is true for us. When we are manic or depressed and suicidal, anxious or paranoid it's much more difficult to get to the root of our problem. As a matter of fact, it may not come across initially that we have BPD because it is overshadowed by the severity of the presenting symptoms. The medication is the bath and food and shelter that's given. It helps to mitigate the more pressing needs and factors so that you can get to a baseline where your core needs can be met.

Medication can be a big part of our lives as people living with mental illness. These medications are prescribed to us to alleviate our more severe and persistent symptoms. Your doctors are concerned with bringing you to a baseline so that you can function well enough to live independently (or your own version of that) and cope with presenting life stressors. Once this has been achieved, therapy will kick in and address your core needs on a deeper level. One big thing to consider is that your concern is not necessarily your doctors' concerns. For example, as you may know all medications have side effects, the most common of those for psychotropic medication is weight gain. My doctors would have prescribed me a certain anti-psychotic because what I was experiencing at the time was racing thoughts and what is known as psychotic depression (depression that is accompanied by psychotic features such as hallucinations, delusion and dissociation). This medication however made me gain 15 pounds in the space of 3 weeks. I then began to spiral even more. The weight gain was not just about a slight discomfort but an aversion to "being like my mother", it was tied to a very deep seeded problem of being shamed for my weight by others but more specifically by my mother. Being "fat" was a huge problem for me psychologically; the weight of that reality was not something I could bear. As a result, I became more depressed - preoccupied with weight gain and weight loss. I exercised multiple times a day, cut back on my food intake and calorie intake but nothing worked. No matter what I cut out or cut down on or how much I exercised, the weight did not budge. I had spoken to the doctors about it and their response was that they deemed that the benefits of the medication outweighed the negative side effects of weight gain. They encouraged me to keep exercising and maintain a healthy diet. Believe me, I tried. The negative for me outweighed the positive. I knew that the weight gain was doing an even bigger number on my mental health than anything else I was facing. I could fight suicidal thoughts but fighting suicide while believing that I was now worth even less because I was fat was beyond me. At that point, I decided that if they refused to try me on a different medication, one that was more weight neutral, I would stop the medication altogether.

My point here is not to give your doctors ultimatums, nor is it to encourage you not to deal with the bigger issue (in this case, why weight gain was an issue for me). The point is our concerns as patients are often not aligned with their concern as doctors. They wanted me to not take my life, that meant more to them than gaining some extra pounds. They were not aware of the level of distress the weight gain caused and figured that it could be worked out in therapy - that way, I could have intervention from different angles. Only I knew and considered that weight gain could be the very thing that pushed me over the edge. I'm not trying to give the doctors flack for not listening rather pointing out that patient concerns are different and should be considered. So, when you are given medication, it is crucial for you to consider what's important to you and how the medication can affect that.

Things To Consider

If you are a person who doesn't like taking medication or has *allergic reactions* to certain chemicals, chances are you may consider not using medication at all. If this is the case, then you must consider long-lasting and impactful alternatives. This means that whatever you decide to do has to be incorporated into your lifestyle. For instance, "mindfulness meditation" is a great way to help bring calm and clarity. Additionally, exercise helps to increase serotonin, endorphins and even dopamine – all of which aid in positive moods. But to create a lasting effect, you would need to practice these regularly. Mindfulness can also help rewire the brain and lessen the effects of depression, anxiety, and survival mode/trauma responses. Again, practices such as these must be consistent to yield any significant result.

You may also want to consider that the borderline brain loves *routine*. The safety that routine creates is very helpful in avoiding being overwhelmed with change and emotional fluidity. Establishing a routine is going to be paramount, especially if you have decided not to take medication or are considering the same. Obviously, I'm talking about a healthy routine which includes socializing (connecting with your support system), exercise, diet, meditation, sleep - and the last includes a time to put your phone down for the night, a nighttime care routine and going to bed at the same time each night (even weekends). I am very aware how daunting and restrictive that sounds, but it is helpful, even more so if you're not on medication.

If you are willing to comply with the medication, a routine is still helpful but something you want to consider is how you feel about weight gain. Really you want to consider all *side effects* of your medication and be aware that each medication can potentially give you different side effects. I mentioned weight gain simply because it is one of the most common side effects of both antidepressants and anti-psychotics. If you are sensitive to that, you may want to take the time to research the medications and try the more weight neutral medications. The downside is that they too have side effects which you then must weigh out. For instance, I was on a well-known antidepressant that is known to cause **weight loss**, however, it made me constantly agitated and angry. I felt no other emotion than a heightened sense of anger, all the time, for no reason. It was torture. So that medication was not suited for me.

SIDE NOTE: If you choose to use a vitamin/supplement instead of medication, also be aware of those side effects. St. John's Wort is a commonly suggested supplement to help with depression and mood. There are several side effects but for me, the blurred vision was affecting my ability to function at work. It didn't actually yield any significant results for me, and the blurred vision was debilitating. My doctor, who prescribed it though, was confident of its positive effects because it worked for her. Which catapults us to my other WARNING:

medications affect people differently. Avoid getting caught up on the Reddit posts, chats and discussion groups about side effects. The medication is likely to affect you differently. Relying on another person's experience is a sure way to be disappointed and could potentially stop you from receiving help that could be beneficial.

This leads me to the other thing to consider. Medication is a *trial-and-error* kind of situation. It can get very tiring. You may end up having to try several different combinations of medications and different types of medication (SSRI's, SNRI's, MAOI's, 1st and 2nd generation anti-psychotics, mood stabilizers, anti-seizure etc.). Also, based on the results you may end up on more medication than you expected or desire to be on. I was once on a combination of an antidepressant and anti-psychotic that was really helping my mind but then I developed involuntary movements in my face – which is called tardive dyskinesia. I then ended up on another medication to help that. Around the same time, I got physically ill and was on some antibiotics which had to be carefully chosen to not disturb the primary medication. I ended up on six different medications at the same time - not fun. Physical illness aside, I was not happy to go from taking one medication to now a steady concoction of three. The point here is that you will have to be patient as you try out different medications and see how they work for you.

Another important thing to consider is price and accessibility. The interesting thing about accessibility is that it differs depending on where you live. Living on an island, it can be difficult to get medications if the supply shortage is island wide. The reason price exacerbated this problem was because I usually purchased medication at the public mental health clinic at a cheaper/subsidized cost. However; when supply is short the focus is on inpatients, so outpatients must fend for themselves by finding their own medication. The prices from private pharmacies are usually three, four or five times the price of a public clinic - and I'm talking about generic medication (this is based on the price of paroxetine [generic for Paxil] in the public clinic which is around $5 while in the private pharmacy is around $30). When I started my medication journey, I took generic sertraline, brand name Zoloft. In the public clinic, a month's supply was around $15.00. When the shortage began, I had to buy from private pharmacies, and it increased to $30.00. This was still manageable. I was not certain what had happened then but when I went back to the public clinic, they started giving me the sample boxes of the brand Zoloft (yes, I did pay for it, and yes, that's technically illegal). However, the cost was the same. When they ran out and I had to get it privately, a month's supply of the brand Zoloft was $80.00 USD. I could not afford it. I went a few days without it and checked every public clinic on the island and could not get it. I found out that the generic version of the medication was no longer being supplied, only the brand. Because of this, the public clinics could not stalk up on them as normal and had to supply only to the inpatients, so all outpatients were left to buy the brand from private pharmacies which was not as affordable. I ended up having to switch medications completely. I use that example to say that not only do you have to be aware of the medications you take but also aware of their availability in your area and the price. If you are on a medication that you cannot afford, or cannot gain access to, you may end up having to switch medications altogether which adds extra time to that trial-and-error period. On the bright side, if the medication is accessible but not affordable, you may be able to tap into a program to assist you in purchasing the medication.

The last thing I want to mention regarding consideration is *general functioning*. As I mentioned earlier, I was on a particular medication that made me exceptionally irritable. I have also been on medication that made me feel like a zombie the following day or so very sleepy that it made me unable to function. Functioning is so important. We must live in the real world just the same as everyone else, which means we have jobs to go to, work to do, children to care for, spouses/significant others to connect with and the like. If we are unable to function because of medication side effects, it leaves us and the people around us at a disadvantage. Imagine having a child who is celebrating winning a championship, but you cannot even feign a smile. The emotional damage incurred is unmatched. Perhaps you have something important to do at work and you can barely move, which can be exacerbated if you perhaps work in customer service. Functioning is vital in being a productive person. Despite if the medication is working, you want to be able to function within all settings. It may be worth it to talk to your doctor about tweaking the dosage or having a different combination altogether. This is not a blanket statement, if your functioning is impacted but it is bearable or wears off before a significant part of your day, you may find that you are fine with the slight impairment.

RECAP: Remember that your concerns about medications are not necessarily the concerns of your doctor. You must be aware of what your concerns are so that you can make an informed decision about how to approach your medical journey. If you decide not to use medication at all, you MUST have a plan to mediate any symptoms you may have. Meditation, exercise, routine et cetera are all things you want to consider for helping you to cope. Please remember that medication is trial-and-error and needs patience and understanding. Be aware of the side effects but do not get too caught up in online forums. Also remember functioning is important and if your functioning is impaired you may need to talk to your doctor about that. Lastly, accessibility and affordability are going to be very important, especially if you live in a rural area. If pricing is an issue, talk to your doctor about how you can tap into social services to assist you.

Chapter 3:

TREATMENT AND THERAPY

Now that we have covered the topic of medication, we are going to cover the next topic that will likely be a long-standing part of your life. Therapy! This is going to be so important to your life as a diagnosed Borderline that I don't have the words to stress it enough. As I mentioned before, medication helps symptoms, but it does not necessarily address the root of the problem. To clarify, there are chemical imbalances in the brain and medication will address those and help to create a balance and level of functioning, but for other symptoms like unstable self-image, or feelings of emptiness, medication won't be able to address those. Those issues are addressed by your friendly neighborhood therapist. Borderline Personality took years to develop, and it will take a while to unravel, unlearn, relearn and manage. The same way a great oak tree takes many years to build its layers, thickness and height; it takes a lot of work and effort to prune it and/or cut it down and foster regrowth. Years of trauma, negative self-talk, and neglect have compounded to create BPD in us. It takes great effort and intention to unlearn that and replace it with positive affirmations, self-worth and security.

When approaching therapy, one thing you may want to consider is the sub-type of Borderline Personality that you best fit in (remember that you may fit into several different categories). I say this because I have found that different types of therapy have different impacts; thus, a specific type may or may not be helpful. For instance, I spent roughly ten years, on and off, doing cognitive behavioral therapy (CBT) with little to no results. There are two major factors that made CBT an ineffective treatment for me. The focus was on identifying and re-framing my thoughts (called cognitive distortions). There was little progress in learning and creating boundaries, no progress in dealing with my sexual abuse history, no progress in developing a stable sense of self and little progress in dealing with my depression/persistent depressive symptoms. Dealing with my cognition was ineffective because I knew the distortions, but trauma made me react in ways that were contrary to what I knew to be true. CBT is an effective treatment for anxiety and depression, but it lacked the techniques needed to address my trauma history and my narcissistic abuse. No matter how much therapy I was receiving or how frequent, without the root of the problem being properly addressed, I could not see significant progress and would wind up right back in the therapy chair. The second reason being that professional rapport was seldom built or prioritized, I rarely felt comfortable with my therapist.

In the Bahamas, if you're using government services to carry out talk therapy (which is the only type that is offered with public services), you only have the option of using the person whom you are assigned. Therefore, there is some rapport building for the sake of building a professional relationship, but not for the sake of ensuring your comfort. You have no choice but to work with who and what you're given. To be fair, in theory, you have an option of switching therapists, but the truth is the department is understaffed and finding another therapist willing to take yet another client is slim. Furthermore, you may end up with a therapist who is unwilling to refer you, even at your request.

When I was first hospitalized and diagnosed, I was assigned a therapist that I was not particularly comfortable with. I was eager to get out of her care after only two weeks but decided to give it more time as a therapeutic relationship takes time and I was probably being a bit paranoid about her intentions. Months into the sessions, I became increasingly frustrated. She frequently misunderstood me and my trying to clarify only made her double down on why she wasn't exactly wrong; this just made me learn not to correct her. Since I couldn't correct her, I learned not to trust her with my authentic self because she would likely misunderstand me, and it would be heartbreaking to have some part of me walked on. I could not be myself and I did not feel safe, this was making me sadder, annoyed, irritated and anxious. Nearing the end of our time, I tried to explain to her (in a letter), that I had been being less than truthful and authentic, also that I felt we should take more time to truly get to know each other and try therapy under better circumstances. The anxiety of how this letter may have been taken as well as what was going on in my life at the time brought me back to self-harm. When I returned to therapy the following week, she didn't bring up the letter and when I asked about it, she accused me of attention seeking. She said that she "found it ironic that you [I] waited until the end of our sessions to give me [the therapist] this letter". She asserted that I had harmed myself to cement that I needed more therapy which played into my fear of abandonment. Hurt is an understatement of what I felt when she said that to me. I couldn't wrap my head around the idea that she would think that I would want to extend my time with someone that I was not having a good time with in the first place. This obviously meant she thought she was great and that I just wanted more time with her, which was so very far from the truth. I asked for a referral to another psychologist, and she told me plainly that she would not refer me to anyone else and if I wanted another therapist within the organization, I would have to find one myself. This ended in many failed attempts to speak to one of the other professionals. When I did happen to speak to another therapist in that organization – which was much later - I was told that I had to keep the therapist I was assigned because it was "better" for continuity. When I explained to that person that my assigned therapist and I didn't have good rapport, I, the client/patient, was instructed to create and maintain rapport because unless the person I was assigned was unethical in some way, I would not be allowed to change.

My point here is that your therapist and therapeutic relationship is of utmost importance to your development, therefore, the relationship must feel secure. If you are not comfortable – whether it is because you don't feel safe, rapport is not substantiated, you don't feel you are progressing or for any other reason - it can hinder your mental health journey.

The reason I say that you should consider your sub-type is because it can affect the type of therapy you need. As a "quiet" borderline, I have trauma and a history of abuse that turns my emotions inward, therefore, trauma therapy and Dialectical Behavior Therapy (DBT) are important. Dialectical Behavior Therapy, mindfulness or anything that focuses on emotional regulation will be absolutely essential for an impulsive borderline (granted it's important for any and every sub-type). Substance abuse therapy may be needed depending on your circumstances as well. One has to be very aware of their needs in order to get the right therapy.

Having said all of that, you must consider the different types of therapy, even those that are unconventional. In the Bahamas, we are not on the cutting edge of treatment and our accessibility to certain types of treatment are non-existent. However, if the treatments and therapies are available to you, take advantage of them and advocate for them where possible. The drug Esketamine is currently undergoing research and is said to help patients with BPD and treatment resistant depression. The intranasal spray Oxytocin is also noted to be useful for BPD patients as it helps with hormonal imbalance. Eye Movement Desensitization and Reprocessing (EMDR) is much easier on the therapist as well as the client and still digs very deep as it relates to trauma. Art therapy is great for emotional regulation and promotes a general healthy lifestyle and creativity. Inner Child work is also exceptionally helpful because of the long-standing complications with childhood trauma. The point is that there are many different types of therapies, and they all have different focuses and impact us in many different ways. You do not need to settle for just talk therapy or just CBT. Keep in mind that if you have decided not to take medication, therapy is that much more important. Having Borderline Personality, therapy should be a regular and consistent part of your journey to help with emotional regulation and persistent depressive symptoms. Since your healing journey is long term, you should settle for nothing less than the best, nothing less than what works best for you.

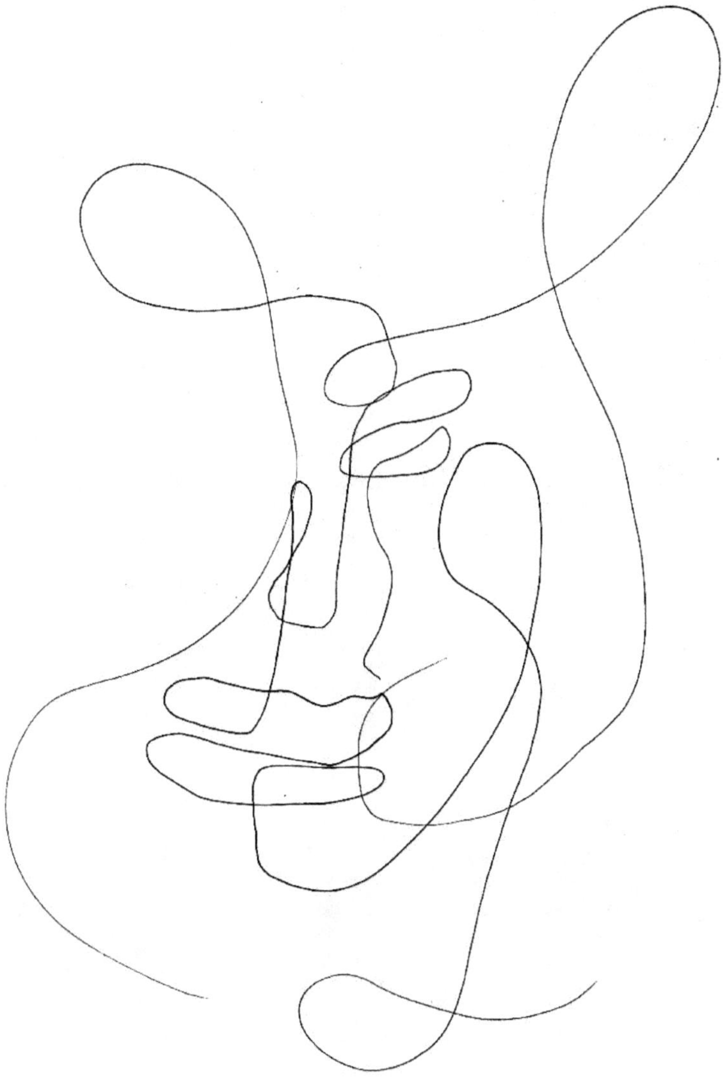

Section 2:

LESS SPOKEN OF CHALLENGES

Chapter 4:

PERSISTENT DEPRESSIVE SYMPTOMS

As I mentioned before, BPD is frequently misdiagnosed as depression (mostly in quiet BPD) and the reason this happens is because of the built-in depressive symptoms. One of the common traits of BPD is the unstable sense of self as well as chronic feelings of emptiness. The operative word being chronic. There is ALWAYS the presence of depression; some level of sadness. There is no real issue with this other than the fact that some professionals miss the chronic nature of BPD. Major Depressive Disorder (MDD), even if it is recurrent, is different and can be addressed and managed. The feelings of sadness, lethargy, lack of motivation, hopelessness, helplessness and general dysphoria are present in MDD and can be mitigated systematically. BPD on the other hand, has lasting symptoms of emptiness, lack of purpose, longing, unstable self-image and not knowing who one really is. Those symptoms are always there in varying levels and thus cannot be treated the same way. Nevertheless, these are the symptoms you will have to become accustomed to managing for a large chunk of your life, if not all of your life.

I wish I was here to tell you that there's a way around this or that there was some trick to ensure that you get the best results in this part of your journey but I'm not. The persistent depressive symptoms are one of the most annoying and distressing parts of the journey. Many days I grappled with the idea that I could spend my entire life never really feeling fulfilled. No one wants to think that they'll spend 50-70 years being unhappy. Now let's put into perspective that for a large number of persons with BPD, they will go into remission after about 10 years and who's symptoms subside as they get older. It is a great accomplishment for those who have experienced this. I am happy for them and wish them all well because the amount of pain that they have endured with this disorder is beyond comprehension for most people. I can only imagine the joys of being free from that, even if they still need occasional therapy or coaching to move past certain obstacles. However, for you who may have only recently been diagnosed, or who may not fall into that lucky group of people, *we* have to deal with these feelings.

What I am here to tell you about these emotions is that they can be managed. One of the common thoughts as it pertains to sadness or lack of self-worth is that you are flawed and though you desire love, it would be unfair to have the person you like to have to deal with you and your chaotic behavior. Another is the constant guilt of seeing yourself make destructive or harmful decisions knowing that you shouldn't have made them but could not stop yourself from doing it anyway. DBT is a great way to tackle the intensity of emotion that comes with feeling this way or thinking these thoughts. Inner-child work is also amazing at helping to reprogram the way you think about yourself and the challenges you face now as a result of your upbringing. These symptoms are those that linger with you for years, those that people tend to overlook. One of the greatest challenges with these emotions is not necessarily the pain of the emotion itself but the many things that surround it.

Often times with chronic conditions people tend to think that because you live with them it means that it's bearable and that you're used to it. They view it the way we view grief. People see it as something that can be debilitating only during the onset and after some time has passed, we learn to live with it and cope. Unfortunately, it's more like having constant phantom pains from a lost limb. It feels like an itch that can't be scratched, a pain that can't be soothed, a cramp that can't be stretched and you feel it ALL THE TIME. No matter how long you've had depressive thoughts, you never get used to being sad all the time. No matter how many suicidal thoughts or even attempts you've experienced, you don't get used to the deep sorrow of feeling you want to end your life. You learn to mask the symptoms so that you don't alarm those around you, but overall, there is no comfort in this level of sadness for extended periods of time.

The joint challenge here is that sometimes you express this sadness and after a time people begin to assume that you just don't WANT to be happy. I cannot tell you the number of times I've heard the comments revolving around "just speak positively, envision a better life, just get up and get out" ...or just about anything that starts with "just do..." Here's an analogy: I don't know how to build a rocket. If a scientist came and laid all the materials in front of me and told me that I now have the tools, resources and materials I need to build the rocket, I still wouldn't be able to do it. If they then gave me a diagram of what it should look like, I'd still mess it up. If they gave me step-by-step instructions, I can still guarantee that something will be off or wrong. Similarly, if I broke my leg, and I were given a splint, wood and bandages, I would still make a complete mess of trying to fix my leg back. Does it mean that I don't want my leg fixed? Absolutely not! I would love to not have a broken leg, but I am unable to do the job. That is what the "just do..." people are like. They assume that if you just do this or just do that, you'll be fixed - if you wanted to. If you choose not to then it means that you don't want to be "fixed". You would not ask someone in a body cast to run a marathon, or a blind person to read a visual sign. However, because our illness is chronic and invisible, there's an assumption that we should and do have the capacity to do things that we just do not. Like myself, I'm sure you've all tried thinking positive, going to the gym, even drinking or smoking or anything to help manage the pain. Unfortunately, our leg has been broken since childhood, and we learned to hobble to deal with the pain. The healed bone is our personality, but it didn't heal properly. Now as adults you're asking us to walk straight. We cannot!

Another set of challenges you deal with regarding persistent depressive symptoms is that people get used to your being sad and so decide not to take you seriously. The challenge with that is that we feel these emotions intensely and it wouldn't be known where on the line we actually fall. For example, I struggle with suicidal thoughts and tendencies and so I tend not to say anything to anyone unless I'm reaching a point where I'm concerned that the thoughts are too frequent and harder to ignore. However, this may happen two or three times per year (depending on what is happening in my life). As a result, someone close to me hears that and thinks that I can't possibly be serious because I just said it 3-4 months ago and nothing happened. Once, I had a "friend" tell me that if I really wanted to die, I would have killed myself by now, therefore he refused to take me seriously. At another point, after a depression screening and finding out that I was severely depressed, a "friend" asked me if I agreed with and was sure of the results because I didn't seem depressed. One of those times I ended up attempting suicide and the other time I had already begun cutting my wrists for relief. People tend not to realize that no matter how much or how often you experience suicidal thoughts, they are not able to accurately gauge how serious the matter is. Although you may have experienced this before, you never know which time will be the time that pushes you over the edge.

TIPS:

The most important thing you need to know about having a naturally low emotional baseline is that it can be managed. Having a low baseline means that you are more prone to feeling sad, depressed, living in the guilt or shame of your responses or generally having an imbalance of your "happy" hormones/chemicals. Although you may not be able to fully get away from the intense emotions or emptiness or the roller coaster ride of self-image, there are things that can be done to make your journey a little bit more palatable. One of those things is *sustainable self-expression.* Often people tend to run to more healthy coping mechanisms when they cannot take it anymore and absolutely need a way to escape or express themselves. At this point is when they reach for the paintbrush or decide to go for a run and as soon as they feel a bit better, or even more so, if things get a bit worse, they stop. Having BPD and having a low baseline for mood and/or functioning, it's imperative to have a strategy that is sustainable. I love art. I love drawing. I can handle myself with charcoal and pastels, a little less a paintbrush, but I'm fairly okay at it. But for a long time, it wasn't sustainable for me. Buying the material to draw or paint was out of reach for me and my pockets and so I had to find an alternative means of expression. I dabbled in creative writing and I liked it but it wasn't something I wanted to do consistently. I would collect and press flowers but that was also not my cup of tea. I absolutely hate running - but that is what stuck with me most. It was free, it led me to see beautiful landscapes, it helped make me tired - thus helping my sleep, it helped me to think in a linear fashion and there was the benefit of weight loss and maintenance. There are tons of research behind why art, writing, exercise and meditation are good for depression but I choose to focus on the fact that they are sustainable. These activities help to maintain an elevated baseline that aids in your functioning and overall well-being.

REMEMBER: Finding your sustainable activity may take time. It's only fair to give each activity a fair chance and that means trying them out for a while to see what you like. I've never liked running, and even though I do it, I still don't like it, but I look forward to the experience I get from running. If I had stopped, just because I didn't like the act of running, I would've missed out on all the benefits. Also be aware of the feelings attached to each activity. Although I love art, before I get to the point of freedom in the craft, I have to get through the feeling of anxiety that I'm not doing it right or messing up some line or the proportions. Having those feelings are fine but take note of them so that you are aware of what you need to work through and whether or not you feel the end feeling is worth pushing through on the front end.

The next tip is *Therapy*. I know I mentioned therapy before and said that it is imperative but what I want to mention here is the importance of therapies that address root/core issues. BPD can develop in the absence of trauma, however, for those of us that have grown up in traumatic environments it is important that we unlearn the toxic thought patterns we developed, learn new ones and relearn our genuine selves. For those of us who have not grown up in traumatic households the exact same applies. BPD affects the way we see ourselves and the way we interact with the world and that means, technically, that our vision is a bit blurred. That being the case, we have to be fitted with prescription glasses tailored for our personal use and adjust to seeing the world in a new way. Just like wearing glasses there are other adjustments to be made - our vision may be corrected but the lenses can sometimes get scratched, they can get foggy in certain weather, it can be hard to see in other types of weather and it can even be annoying to keep on your face all the time. Despite all the challenges that come with wearing glasses, the alternative of not wearing them and not being able to see clearly at all is not as enticing. Inner child work, trauma therapy, art trauma therapy, and DBT are all recommended to help adjust our actions and feelings and help elevate our overall baseline.

REMEMBER: There will be challenges. You may need some string to keep those glasses on and even still there are other issues that may impair your vision sometimes, but it doesn't mean that there isn't hope at all, it doesn't mean that life without glasses was better. In George Orwell's Animal Farm, despite overthrowing the human leadership and being run by an all-animal leadership the animals ended up in the same if not a worse condition. This is not Animal Farm. Despite having different challenges, namely falling back into an old habit, dealing with the guilt/shame of past relationships or behaviors and so forth it's easier to get back on the horse and try again. It's easier to wipe off those glasses, to change the lenses or even upgrade the lenses and get back to a healthier way of living. You have to give yourself room to learn, to adjust, to make mistakes and to try again.

My last tip is *consistent self-care - specifically grace.* Self-Care is not just the nice things we do for ourselves but also the hard things like setting boundaries, discussing our feelings and being assertive with our needs. When I say self-care, I AM actually talking about the massage and nail polish and hair washing and the list goes on. Grace is defined as unmerited or unearned favor. As Borderlines, I want to push against that. We are in a constant state of thinking that we didn't do anything to deserve the good things we do for ourselves. What I want us to do really is to tell ourselves that we deserve that massage because we had a hard week, because we made it through those intense emotions, because we messed up and tried again, because the guilt we carried about that thing we did was heavy. Self-Care in this instance is to, on a consistent basis, check in with ourselves and take note of all the heavy feelings we've experienced, and all the progress we've made and make room for that to be okay. Make room in your heart and mind for the mistakes and the lessons (learned and unlearned) and treat yourself well or at least kind for having experienced it. Just because you have BPD means you deserve a hug and an ice cream cone, even if you're giving it to yourself. I know that practicing this will not come easy, but it is necessary.

On one occasion this guy I was dating had screwed me over several times but each time I found it in my heart to forgive him. I had many opportunities to cut him off and end my relationship with him, honestly at one point I did. Each time I would look at the effort he made and thought that it was worth giving him another try despite my better judgment telling me not to. Eventually he gave me an STI (a curable one, thankfully) and I had it. I was venting to my friend about how upset I was at myself for having grown up in a home where abuse was normal, and I no longer knew when to listen to myself. I had a list of persons that I would have had a "feeling" about them that made me uneasy or feel like I wasn't safe, and for each of those persons I pushed that feeling aside and continued in the relationship/friendship. Each time I ended up holding the shitty end of the stick. Even though he was clearly in the wrong here I was upset at myself. My friend didn't completely absolve me and validated that I did, in fact, make the wrong decision but I did not give myself any grace for being mentally ill. I gave myself no grace for having grown up in an environment where I had to push aside that feeling of not being safe to cater to my abuser. My friend told me 80% of the blame is on the perpetrator for their behavior, 15% of the blame is on my illness which sets me up to make these decisions and I can choose to take the last 5% of the blame for having not learned to listen to myself if I please. I had zero grace for myself. I refused to believe that anyone else was the problem other than my "broken" self. I needed to be reminded that there is grace for me and my mistakes. There is grace for you too.

Chapter 5:

FEAR OF LONELINESS

The fear of abandonment is a very prominent trait of BPD and the "frantic" attempts to avoid it. There are several ways to break this down when explaining *why* we do this but no matter which way we peel the banana, it reveals the fear of being alone. The most common attachment style of the Borderline is Fearful avoidant/disorganized. This basically means that there is a constant push and pull in the relationship. We desire closeness. We want people to know us and love us and accept us and see us at our core. In the same vein, we are afraid to lose such a person that can or is willing to do so because we don't believe our core is beautiful, we don't feel worthy, and we fear the rejection that comes with someone finding out how "ugly" we really are. Therein lies the pattern - we reel people in, in hopes of finding someone to truly love us, then we loosen the grip in fear that if they get too close, they may leave. This shows up in a variety of ways like self-sabotage, not engaging in activities for fear of being rejected in some way, rejecting others before they can reject you, hiding different layers of yourself etc. We hate the idea that someone can leave us, that we are easy to leave or worth leaving, we hate the implication that if one person (usually your favorite person) leaves, there's a chance that anyone and everyone can leave. This brings light to the idea that what we are afraid of more than the abandonment itself, rather the loneliness that is attached to it.

When a person seems to be pulling away (real or perceived), we think about how no one else will ever love us again, how we are not worthy of love because we are fundamentally flawed and easy to leave. We assume that we will not be able to open up to anyone else the same way, that people are bound to hurt us and even more so that we deserve that hurt. It doesn't matter that the person never treated us right - the fault was ours in one way or the other. It doesn't matter that the person prepared us for the change in the relationship - the onus is on us to make it work, even if we can't. Whether the relationship was good or bad, if we cannot make it work, there is a fear that we will mess up everything with everyone else and we will end up alone and broken. THIS, I think, is the real trouble with "fear of abandonment". We are constantly fighting for someone to stay in our lives because it gives credence to our inherent belief that we are of value; it gives rhyme and reason to our desire to be worthy of connection; it helps us to navigate our worlds' and our minds with a sense of safety. When this is threatened, the fear of traversing the world (that's on fire) alone with open and raw wounds becomes too much to bear.

We all know that there is a difference between being alone and being lonely. I want to stand on a ledge here and say that being alone is not a challenge. In the event that we are overstimulated, we withdraw. In the event of being triggered, we withdraw - and in a healthy way. We can acknowledge that being alone can help us to regroup and tackle the world again. When someone becomes part of that withdrawal process and offers safety in regrouping, losing that person becomes life altering. We all feel this is some way during a breakup. There is a profound grief that accompanies losing that person that you would otherwise lean on to get you through said grief. Our emotional rawness makes this grief even more tender and last for longer periods of time. The fear, grief and loneliness around losing a friend, partner or loved one is not uncommon. It is the idea that these negative emotions point to our unworthiness, our being deserving of the pain, and our reluctance to believe that we can and will build again, that makes the BPD fear of abandonment and fear of loneliness so different.

Another way to address this matter would be to explore sustained emotional neglect. Not everyone that is diagnosed with BPD has a history of trauma or had a traumatic event happen to them. However, I tend to see a pattern of sustained emotional neglect and "micro-trauma". For example, I definitely got "beatings" or "whoopings" as a child. I also received some punishment that was certainly abuse, like being choked to the point of nearly passing out or kicked while on the ground cowering. What I never realized was abuse, was the emotional neglect I was not fully aware I was undergoing. I cannot count the number of times I would ask "why can everyone see the good in me, but she [my mother] can't?" There was a book that I wrote in that acted as my diary where when I re-read it, I was surprised at the number of times I asked, "why is nothing I do ever enough?" As much as I made excuses for my father, whom I thought was a fellow victim of my mother's rage - I would still wonder "why does he choose to be out, go out and save himself and leave us here to suffer?" "Don't we deserve a break too? A place of comfort and relaxation?" The point is, I was consistently and constantly in a place of wondering why I was not enough, trying to prove my worth and my value, I was constantly alone and having to adapt and mold myself into something that was deemed acceptable/tolerable to my ever-changing environment. When I got older, I was in several "situationships" where I was not allowed to be seen with the person in public, I was not allowed to be seen by their family, I was not allowed to even (and this is going to sound preposterous but it's true) dream about their family. These individuals would only show up at night, be upset about the flood lights that betrayed their anonymity or allow me to only come in the dead of night when everyone was either gone or asleep, parked in such a way that I would not be seen and not allowed inside unless there was an all-clear. Although I was aware that it did not feel good and that it broke my heart several ways to Sunday, I was not aware that it was reminiscent of my childhood until one day I heard myself ask "why am I not enough?"

I kept thinking that maybe they would see my value one day, maybe they would realize how I can fit into their lives perfectly, maybe they would realize that I'm not a bad person and I'm worthy of their love. When I asked about "being enough", it was the first time I realized how many persons I had in my life over the course of many years, that were not the best persons to be around. However, I kept fighting for them to love me; I was afraid of them leaving or me leaving them because it somehow proved that I really was never worth it and never will be. Having them exit my life or me exit theirs meant that something truly was inherently wrong with me, and I was not deserving of their love and affection and to a greater degree, I was not worthy of ANYONE'S. The constant "little" (yes, I use quotes because these are not little by any means) traumas are enough to change the way we see ourselves and the way that we interact with the world. Fear of abandonment is also the fear of admitting that we are not worthy of connection and thus deserve to be alone for all eternity. Luckily, that is not the truth!

TIPS:

As a result of these many and repeated traumas we often forget who we are (or that person was never actually developed) and we tend to mold ourselves into versions of ourselves that are acceptable and tolerable to those we're around. Since our personalities are so malleable, it can impact the spaces we find ourselves in and how we feel about those spaces. What I mean by that is we tend to fit fairly well into most and many spaces, and in those spaces, we are not fully comfortable because we are not certain if the space is one we chose and want or one we fit into without any real desire to be there. We can then become resentful of the persons in that space, we can sabotage the relationship or the community as a result of feeling and living like an outsider or we can feel very empty and not useful in that space and shrink, tense up or avoid interactions completely. The best thing we can do for this is to explore the concepts in *inner child work.* Inner child work can help you to revisit and re-parent that inner child that was forced to be someone they were not in order to be tolerated by a parent or caregiver. It can help you to revisit feelings you never got to explore because of shame and abuse and thus discover the things you truly wanted to do and take part in. Inner child work is a great way to help to build up your sense of self and by extension you know who you are, what you want and how to engage in it without the fear of feeling isolated. You are less likely to sabotage or push people away because you are more comfortable in your own skin and knowing that you are worthy of the connection you receive from like-minded individuals.

Choosing suitable relationships is another key point that can be found in inner child work, DBT, trauma therapy and CBT. All of these therapies use different methods that guide you to a point of stability in choosing relationships that are healthy and sustainable. CBT helps you to pinpoint maladaptive thinking patterns and address them in active relationships. DBT focuses on interpersonal relationships and how to create boundaries around yourself and others so that you can exercise distress tolerance and emotional regulation. Trauma therapies take you back to the root of the problem and help you to build on principles that combat the thought processes developed as a result of the faulty settings of trauma. The point here is that once you address your challenges, you can then choose relationships that are conducive to your overall well-being. This is important because you will now have relationships built on stability and do not reinforce the premise that you are unworthy and undeserving of love. In the example I mentioned above, all of those relationships I held all reinforced that I was not enough, that I was not worth the effort it took to truly be part of their lives, that I was undeserving of being incorporated into their realities. When we continue to choose relationships - friendships and otherwise - that reinforce the idea that we already fear, the loneliness that is dredged up becomes unbearable and the fear of abandonment becomes inevitable. Fear of abandonment lessens when there is security in the relationship, as it was built on mutual trust and understanding. In the presence of this stability feelings of loneliness diminish.

The last and most daunting thing I want to mention, and this ties into both inner child work and choosing stable relationships, is the *gradual testing of vulnerability.* When we are learning who we are, and building community around that, we will eventually get to a point where the persons we are building with will be tested. THIS is different from the self-sabotage testing that is common among people with BPD. Sabotage in this way is when we are in need in some way and then we say it to the person in question and wait to see if they will give you the response you were looking for, and when they don't it becomes a reason to not trust them; to push them away; to reinforce why you are not important. THAT IS NOT WHAT I MEAN BY TESTING!!! I was part of a polyamorous relationship once. One day I was not doing well and needed some company. I drove to a beach that was near my partner's home and told them I was there. I was asked if I wanted them to come to which I responded something along the lines of you don't have to if you it's too much for you. When they didn't show up, I was literally devastated because that meant, to me, that I would never be chosen first and I would never be their priority, and I was not as important to them as the other person or as they were to me. That was not a fair test. A fair test would have been when I was asked, I responded with I would really appreciate the company. If at that point a decision was made not to come and sit with me, I could make an assumption that perhaps I was not as much of a priority in their life. I say perhaps because that would not factor in any outstanding variables like an emergency, or a call in to work, or something else of great importance. We cannot test people without giving them information with which to act first.

Testing in this case would mean setting a boundary clearly between two parties and allowing the other party to respect or reject that boundary. If the boundary is respected then you have the ability to allow the person into more "protected" areas of your life and slowly peel away the layers of yourself. If the boundary is rejected, you have the ability to talk about it openly and decide whether or not you feel comfortable allowing the person to get another chance or to walk away from the relationship. The mutual testing of boundaries and vulnerability is key in creating spaces where there is trust that abandonment will not be the first or inevitable course of action. Again, alleviating the pressure felt by the fear of abandonment, diminishes the fear of walking through life alone.

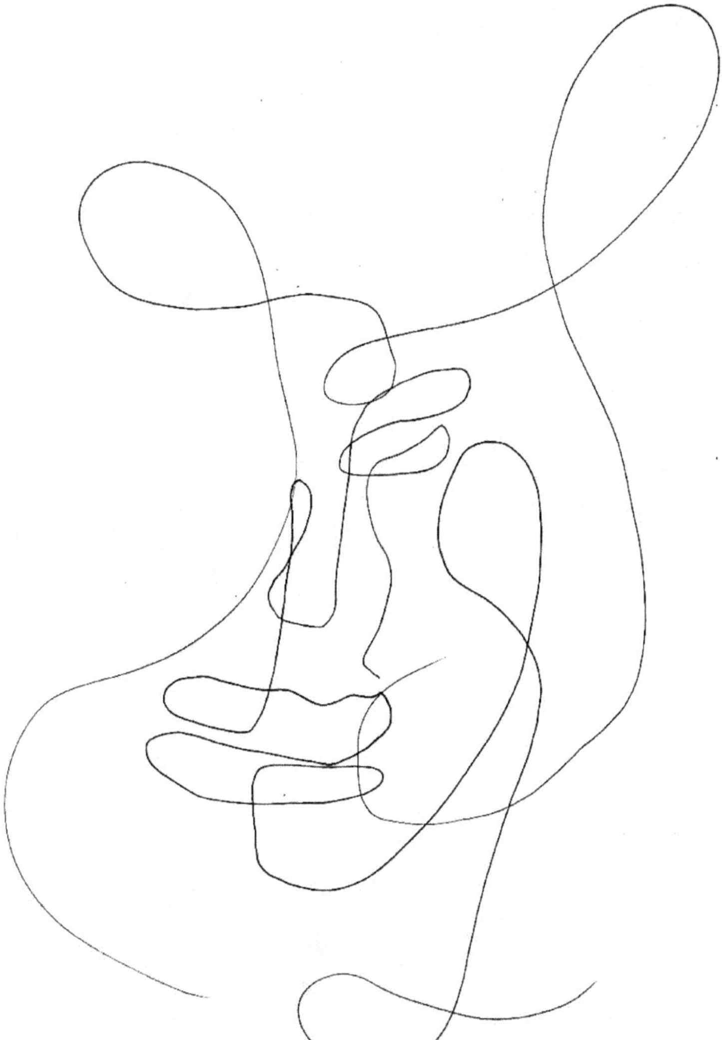

Section 3:

MANAGING RELATIONSHIPS

Chapter 6:

THE IMPACT OF (TRAUMA) THERAPY IN RELATIONSHIPS

Over the last few years, I've spent a great deal of time researching Narcissistic Personality Disorder (NPD) and narcissistic personality traits, as I came to the slow and disheartening realization that I had filled my life with people who possessed these traits. I grew up in a home where at least one of my parents was narcissistic and the other was at least an enabler, if not both being narcissistic. I only came to realize this when my first and only (at the time) real relationship came to a head, and I had no other choice but to realize that they had Narcissistic Personality Disorder and I was enduring narcissistic abuse. This was particularly significant because this partner reminded me of my parents – which led to my making important connections. As I started to pull away from my romantic relationship, I saw how trapped I was in the same cycle with my parent. The more I dissected my childhood, the more I realized that narcissistic abuse was my norm. I did not know anything else. As a result, I filled my life with characters that gave a familiar feeling and a familiar abuse. My (then) spiritual community was infamous for communal narcissism, and the persons the community attracted were either used to being on the receiving or giving end of abuse themselves. This means that my "friends" all had these traits to varying degrees and it became obvious to me that I had truly surrounded myself with very toxic individuals.

I don't blame myself for this (at least not entirely). I had been raised by predators therefore attracting other predators was just part of the job. Despite the fact I did not fit in and was uncomfortable in many ways in these environments, I had accepted this lot in life. I did not challenge these people or their behaviors and beliefs, even when the discomfort felt unbearable and led to crippling depression. At different points when I did challenge them I would "fold" and accept that I was the more likely perpetrator of some evil or wrongdoing. The actual challenge came when I sincerely connected with someone who was NOT a predator. This person was clean air amidst smoke. Naturally, I took a deep breath and refused to let it out. With their help I was able to leave my spiritual community, move out from my emotionally abusive parents' household, create distance between and even drop some of my unhealthy friendships and create a clean space for me. The only problem was that I dropped all these things, not replaced them. Imagine having a home and it's full of all sorts of furniture, knick-knacks, clothes, dishes and the like. One by one, piece by piece you sell everything in the house but the sofa. You begin to eat on the sofa, sleep on the sofa, work on the sofa, relax on the sofa, stress on the sofa, cry on the sofa, sit on the sofa, lay on the sofa, you do everything on the sofa…until the sofa becomes worn out and can no longer hold your weight. This tendency to allow one person to define your entire world is what is known in most BPD literature as the "favorite person" problem. I can argue that my case was a bit different because your favorite person can and usually does exist within the context of other people and communities being present. The premise of having one person that means more to you than anyone else in the world still remains. Most people with Borderline Personality Disorder have experienced a significant amount of trauma and abuse in their childhood years. The persistent presence of this trauma causes our brains to conform into believing that the world is dangerous ALL THE TIME and thus creating a personality that interacts with the world based on that belief. Therefore, armed with the reinforced belief that the world is not safe, when you find someone that feels safe you latch onto them.

This is where attachment styles come into play. People with BPD tend to lean toward having "Fearful-Avoidant/Disorganized" attachment styles. The dynamic is a natural push-pull relationship. You may have heard the phrase "I hate you, don't leave me" in regards to Borderline Personality. There is a desire to love and empathize with others, a desire for connection and intimacy, but that exists alongside an understandable hesitation to let others in for fear of being hurt or abandoned. This is not to say that a fearful avoidant or disorganized attachment style is the only possibility but the point I'm making here is that our wounds and trauma are key factors of the health of our relationships in adulthood. The borderline individual happens to have a very extreme way of showing the unhealthy patterns that develop as a result of unhealthy attachment styles in childhood. This becomes the reason trauma therapy and inner-child work becomes so invaluable in the treatment of BPD. DBT therapy also has an amazing way of helping us to get to the "mother wound" and addressing how and why we developed the attachment styles that we have and display. When we tackle the root of the issue, it leaves us in a place where we are better able to express our needs, desires, expectations, disappointments and emotions.

The challenge with my writing this is that at the time of this publication, I have yet to master healthy or secure attachment. I cannot, with any degree of confidence, give you advice about maintaining healthy relationships. What I can tell you though, is that I have found that the healthier I am, the better my relationships tend to be. The example I gave in the beginning of this chapter about the relationship that helped me to get rid of so many unhealthy things came on the heels of my working toward sustaining a healthy relationship with myself. At the time I connected with this friend I was exercising consistently; I had lost a significant amount of weight that I had gained through stress and I was feeling comfortable in my body; I was in the process of revamping friendships and relationships; limiting screen time; utilizing an emotion wheel; consistent with my sleep hygiene and I began seeing a therapist (using narrative therapy). I was a healthier version of myself, and their presence added to my happiness. The problem arose when therapy ended (not for any fault of the therapist) without my having gotten to the root of my issues, the "mother wound". I kept stripping away things that were unhealthy without addressing the root problem which for me was safety or lack thereof. I also stopped adding spaces where I felt safe and at peace. My safe spaces rapidly shifted from being dilapidated to being non-existent, leading to a complete mental break. For you the challenge may be support, or abandonment, or authenticity, family or any number of things/triggers. When we do not learn how to address the major wound, we become more prone to repeating the mistake with others.

Indulge me for a second with another fairly dark analogy. Imagine being in a car accident. There is blood everywhere! There are cuts all along your arms, your legs, about your body, a large gash in your head and possibly some internal bleeding. When EMS comes, they start to clean you up, removing the broken shards of glass, putting bandages on wounds and cleaning up the manageable wounds. When you get to the doctors, they stitch up your head wound, and they note that you do have some internal bleeding, but they don't know where the bleeding is coming from. They usher you into the operating room and at just that moment someone comes into the ER that needs immediate attention, and the doctors all rush out and leave you there. You somehow leave and are never operated on. No one is able to see your internal bleeding and your external wounds are healing up very nicely. Only as time goes on and your body starts to take on more strain does the impact of your internal injuries start to become obvious.

We have an internal injury that people are not able to see on the surface. In fact, on the surface we look fairly healthy, with self-help/basic help, we may be healing up nicely. The internal injury will always be the thing that causes us and those around us harm because on it hangs life and death. The life and death of our relationships. We cannot fix the wound unless we know what and where the wound is. Certain changes we make can and will help us, but our health cannot be maintained until the main wound is healed. The blood will continue to fill us to the point of overflow until the internal injury is addressed. This analogy can apply to any mental health challenge, but I want to use this to carry the weight of therapy. Fixing the smaller wounds adds to your overall well-being but not addressing the root still has the capacity to wreak havoc. That healthy relationship I had could have been maintained had I not started coughing up blood all over them. I am nearly certain that you can pinpoint a relationship that started out well and ended up in shambles because you, for one reason or the other, were unable to keep yourself together. Unable, because you were unhealed.

PRO TIP: GO TO THERAPY! STAY IN THERAPY! Going to therapy is only half the battle. Once in therapy you are likely going to encounter some very touchy topics like family, sense of self, abandonment...and those are umbrella topics for all the weighty things that will surface when you talk about these areas of your life. The key is remaining consistent. It's very common to abandon ship when the proverbial "shit" hits the fan in therapy. The knee-jerk reaction is to not want to stick around to clean it up. Therapy is designed to help you see the mess and clean it up. It gives you the tools to keep cleaning as you continue to come across more areas of your life with "shit" smeared on it. As I mentioned, not every therapy is going to be helpful, not every therapist is going to give you what you need but you must be *committed to the process.*

LAST TIP: Therapy is **NOT** the only answer. I realize that this book is very pro therapy. As a mental health professional and therapy client, I believe in the strength and power of therapy. As an Islander, nature lover and spiritual individual, I truly believe that there are other ways you can self-reflect, gain insight and build psychoeducation. I don't advise that you rely too heavily on Tik Tok, Youtube or social media in general for psychoeducation but if you decide, for any reason, that you don't want to have therapy then I encourage you to do what is best for you. If therapy for you is to buy a chihuahua and talk to it, then please do so. If therapy means going hiking and spending time barefooted on the grass or in the sand, then do so. If therapy for you is sitting in a drumming circle, knitting circle, support group, book club, hot yoga or a prayer closet, then by all means, engage in those things. Culture can lead us to believe that therapy is individual and has to take the form of two people sitting across from each other. The purpose of psychoeducation is to help you to understand the wound and equip you with tools to fix it. Get the education and use the tools that are most beneficial and comfortable for you.

Chapter 7:

COMMUNICATING

Communication is important for any relationship, yet the reality of BPD is such that communicating is exceptionally difficult. Based on our push-pull attachment styles; heightened emotions; emotional dysregulation and challenges with identifying emotions, the communication of anything surrounding emotions can be problematic. Although learning to identify, regulate and communicate emotions can be learned independently, in the previous chapter I highlighted the importance of therapy and how it helps to identify and address the "mother wound". Once the wound has been identified and addressed, it will then be of utmost importance to foster healing by creating a community where safety and support can be encouraged and reinforced. The only way to foster the healing (of the "mother wound") and maintain the relationships being built is by communicating your strengths, weaknesses, expectations, desires, needs and disappointments.

One of the most important things I've learned regarding communication is to build the plane while it's on the ground. Trying to fix the wing of the plane while it's flying is arduous and dangerous if not downright impossible. In most cases any issues with the plane are fixed while it's on land, grounded and ideally in the engineer's docking station. In the same way, asking someone in an emotionally heightened state how to help should be a last resort because it is very rarely fruitful, if not an act in futility. Naturally, telling someone to calm down or asking how to help someone in a state of anger or panic is hard because they cannot settle their brain or body enough to search for the answers. I think about an episode of SpongeBob SquarePants where SpongeBob clears his mind of everything not related to fine dining and when he is asked his name his brain catches fire and his subconscious is running around screaming, searching for the information but it's not there. Those of us with Borderline Personality Disorder tend to get triggered by things that most people see as rather small and we get triggered rather "easily" (as others may see it). Once you have been triggered, the plane is in the air, and it will be a bit of a lengthy flight. If you happen to have a co-occurring disorder like depression or bi-polar disorder that has the potential to lead you into a prolonged period of unrest, you can buckle up for an extended trip. Once the plane takes off, trying to fix it is not possible; when the fire has started in our minds and bodies, searching for information is futile.

The point that I'm getting at is that it is best to have these conversations about needs and the like when you are in a state of rest. There is an air of hindsight is 20/20. You are able to access your memory and your prefrontal cortex (which is responsible for logic and reasoning) which allows you the ability to say what is helpful, when it is helpful and signs of when is the most beneficial time to implement the strategies. Trying to access this kind of information when the amygdala (emotional processing) and hypothalamus (fight/flight response) are activated will give you a resounding "I don't know". Beware that "I don't know" is the "clean" version of the possible responses. The part of this that is key is sharing this information with a community of people that can be trusted.

Fixing the plane on the ground is important, and the other part of that is getting the appropriate people to do the work. It is inadvisable to allow people who have not proven themselves as safe spaces to have access to your more vulnerable areas. I mentioned before, relationships are very hard for us because of our attachment styles, childhood traumas and emotional dysregulation.

- Therapy helps us to get to the point of addressing the wounds and learning to identify and foster healthy relationships.
- Once you identify your circle of friends and support, life will provide you with the opportunity to healthily test these relationships.
- Therapy will be at play teaching you the skills to regulate and communicate.

It is imperative that while you are testing relationships (because you will get triggered) you create a safety net where your wounds are not hidden, and your needs are known so that you have a space of support when you are triggered. Initially this may be your therapist, your immediate family or longtime friend. You will then expand this safety net as you learn to trust people with the more vulnerable parts of yourself. I have noticed that with a lot of people that live with BPD, there is a tendency to begin relationships with the telling of very personal and vulnerable details. There are a lot of reasons for this but in essence it can be attached to the push-pull nature of our attachment styles; there is a level of testing that accompanies telling personal details and assessing how one responds to that information. However, doing this allows for an excessive amount of disappointment as people do not know how to respond or react to that information. They have not been "tested" with smaller, more insignificant information nor were they equipped with strategies to help if you become triggered. Not everyone has the skills, the wherewithal or the desire to fix the plane. As the popular adage says, "you cannot judge the intelligence of a fish by its ability to climb a tree."

The last thing I want to mention in this section is the importance of distributing the workload. Therapy teaches you to address the wound so that you can communicate your needs while building healthy relationships. An important part of having relationships is that you need more than one. In the previous chapter I mentioned my having a singular healthy relationship during a time when I was weeding out other unhealthy relationships. I mentioned how easy it can become to rely on one person for the bulk of your interpersonal needs - which is commonly known as the BPD favorite person. This is a very easy trap to fall into for so many reasons including society focusing heavily on romantic relationships and their place in our lives. The favorite person trope really exacerbates the challenges surrounding this concept, placing an unreasonably large responsibility on the favorite person to fulfill the needs of an entire community. Keep in mind that your favorite person may not be a romantic partner but a friend, sibling, coworker or anyone who's presence you value more than others in your life. In healthy relationships, each individual has a hobby of their own, with a community of like-minded people as well as friends and family that come together to meet different needs. Going back to my example - having a dining table alleviates the need to eat on the sofa; having a bed alleviates the need to sleep on the sofa, having a work desk alleviates the need to work on the sofa and so on. When one thing is relied on to fill the need and purpose of many others, it creates an unhealthy dependence on that thing and causes it to become worn out. The same applies to people. If one person is expected to bear the role of spiritual leader/influence, party friend, relaxing friend, hobby friend, venting friend, family member, etc., that person will eventually become overburdened, worn out and burnt out. As a result, they will pull away or handle you without the proper care more and more often which will inevitably cause hurt, disappointment and rage. The community has to be spread out where different people hold different roles and add to your health in a variety of ways. Each of these people will have differing levels of access to your information and can be trusted to provide that which they are responsible for. The goal here is to avoid burn-out in your relationships and to limit the chances of codependency and rage.

I want to tie this together by telling a story. I have a friend that has, over a number of years, invested a lot into our friendship and the closer we got the more they were able to connect the dots of how I felt about certain things. My friend then decided to clearly ask how they could help and went into detail about the weight of the question, as they knew that it was common for me to take on the entire burden of proving that I was worthy of the friendship. They understood the importance of knowing my tendencies to carry burdens while exempting others from having to return the favor. In a time when my house was emptied out of everything and my safe spaces were all gone this friend offered me proverbial shelter. I was able to give basic answers to what I needed but as time went on, I would build on that framework with them. When I later went into a deep depressive state, I did not need to tell them to assist with cooking, or cleaning or presence. It was already known what was important to me and how to offer it. That is the impact of testing appropriately and allowing the plane to be built when the plane is on the ground.

In the same vein another friend connected with me and we helped each other through difficult times sharing our presence among other things. Yet there were instances where I would feel emotionally vulnerable and needing support in that way and I was never able to receive that level of care from them. I realized later that the reason they weren't offering that kind of support was because they were unable to because of their own upbringing and belief system. I likened it to tapping into government services for financial assistance. You would advise them that you are struggling to take care of yourself and need their help. They give you a voucher to go to the store and buy food, but you have no gas or electricity to prepare the food. You are appreciative of the food because you do, in fact, need the food but without yet another essential element you are not in a significantly better position. When I combine the efforts of my first friend that provided shelter and the other that provided grocery, I am now in a better position to take care of myself without requesting either friend to provide more than they are able. The friend that was equipped to fix the plane did just that. The friend that was unable to fix the plane but was able to outfit the interior did just that. The end result is a functional and aesthetically pleasing aircraft.

TIPS:

Build the plane while it's on the ground. Communicating your needs, desires, expectations, and tips on how to help you in times of distress is important to do at times when you have the ability to. When you are in an aroused or even depressed state you are unable to adequately express what it takes to help you. This must be done when you have the cognitive functioning and cognizance to do so. At the point of creating these connections you have the opportunity to test who has the ability to assist and allow them adequate access. You want to only allow people who have proven themselves as an asset and are willing to respect your wounds and your boundaries with the clearance to access the deeper, more vulnerable parts of you. *Only the skilled get the privilege of fixing the plane.* Lastly, you want to ensure that you *build a community.* Relying on one person to hold your whole person together will only end up in hurt feelings, burn out and rage. Having a community of people with differing roles and differing levels of access allows you and the people around you to show up in more meaningful ways with a larger capacity with which to meet those needs.

Conclusion:

EMBARKING ON YOUR MENTAL HEALTH JOURNEY

It is customary to begin a conclusion with "in conclusion" rather, I want to say thank you. Furthermore, I encourage you to say thank you to yourself. You have received and accepted your diagnosis, bought tools to help you through it and read through to the end. You have made so many steps in helping yourself, none of which should be taken for granted or overlooked. There are many difficult things to navigate with the diagnosis of Borderline Personality Disorder. For me, one of them is consistently acknowledging the disorder and the grace I need to give myself. I tend to go about my day - sometimes saying with words that I have BPD but not acknowledging the magnitude of challenges that accompany the disorder. I take on responsibilities and tasks without weighing the impact it could have on my mental health; I enter or begin relationships without counting the cost of the work that I need to put in and in general I tend to treat myself like a "neurotypical" person. There are so many things that I've learned over the years that I cannot find on the internet or are seldom talked about even in BPD circles. That is why I wrote this book. The fact that you have taken a hands-on approach to learning and navigating this challenge is beyond commendable. You are acknowledging your deficit and actively seeking to fill in the blanks. I thank you for breaking the stigma and adding to a community of functional BPD-ers and you should thank yourself for being proactive and responsible.

Hopefully, this book will have taught you a few things that are usually difficult to get support for or talk about. The goal is to open the door for these conversations to happen and to spare you the need to go through certain experiences for you to learn. This is vicarious learning. In the same vein, this is not blanket learning that alleviates the need for other modes of treatment. On the contrary, I encourage therapy, shadow work, trauma treatment, inner child work, spirituality, acupuncture, exercise, self-care and the like. I encourage you to take your mental health into your own hands. What that means is doing the work and being informed about what you are doing and why. This book does not replace your DBT workbook, your mood tracker, your affirmations or your therapy. This book is to give you an insight into challenges associated with BPD and equip you with the resources and tips of how to deal with them.

Borderline Personality Disorder and mental health at large is a lifelong journey. You will always be working; always be growing; and always be learning. There will be times when you get discouraged, disheartened and just downright tired. You won't want to fight. In these times, give yourself a break and give yourself some grace. If you forget you have a disorder and go into a daze, then remember afterward that you don't function the same as everyone else, GIVE YOURSELF A BREAK. If you have a hard time discussing your feelings and you end up feeling isolated and lonely, GIVE YOURSELF SOME GRACE. If you fall short in a relationship because you became a bit fixated on your favorite person, GIVE YOURSELF GRACE. Keep in mind that I'm not saying run away from responsibility or accountability but know that life is hard and requires gentle correction with understanding and empathy. Empathy, understanding and flexibility are your greatest tools. Never underestimate them.

I wish you all the best on your journey and I stand in solidarity with you and all that is to come.

www.ingramcontent.com/pod-product-compliance
Lightning Source LLC
Chambersburg PA
CBHW070645240926
51846CB00003BA/782
9789769756106